T0355038

THE
WELL DRESSED
OLIVE

THE
WELL DRESSED
OLIVE

A TRIP BACK IN TIME AND DREAMS FULFILLED

John M. Noldan

Archway Publishing books may be ordered through booksellers or by contacting:

Archway Publishing
1663 Liberty Drive
Bloomington, IN 47403
www.archwaypublishing.com
844-669-3957

ISBN: 978-1-6657-6525-1 (sc)
ISBN: 978-1-6657-6526-8 (hc)
ISBN: 978-1-6657-6527-5 (e)

Library of Congress Control Number: 2024923228

Print information available on the last page.

Archway Publishing rev. date: 11/13/2024

Dedication

To all those with dreams which become reality and fulfilled. But to those unfulfilled, they are only to be sought after but never realized. Fleeting, recurring visions that are creations of our imagination that drive us thru fantasy. A human experience that makes us all one. Never forget that the eyes are the pathways to one's soul, for better or worse, or richer or poorer…

Forever grateful for my sister Dee whose ability to listen and not judge provided the advice given to me during difficult years as we grew up together facing our troubled youth. She loved those olives so dearly that this one is for her. As happens in life, she sadly left us March 2024 to rest in peace.

Contents

Chapter 1

MY FIRST RECOLLECTIONS OF MY EARLY YEARS ARE the images of lily pads and slow-moving water and the sounds of croaking frogs. I vividly remember the flowing creek and the nearby meadow and swamp that extended over a several-mile area adjacent to my childhood home. I really miss that experience growing up, trying to catch tadpoles and rowing in Dad's old, dilapidated boat, dealing only with the solitude and peace of nature.

I can't stop thinking about that peacefulness that surrounded our old house in southern New Jersey that rested on a small plot of land next to a tidal creek. Its waters moved in and out daily over several hours as I witnessed the rise and fall of the water level. It would expose, at low tide, the mudbanks and the narrow waterway leading out to the Delaware River. Then the cycle would reverse itself over hours, with the high-water mark of the creek at times nearing the top of its banks without overflowing. On a warm day, with the effects of the heat and the low tide, the unpleasant, stale stench emitted by the sun-baking mud and whatever had decomposed would offend some, but not me and my family. It was like a perfume that only boaters and fishermen and creek dwellers could appreciate and become invigorated from being so close to nature.

Unfortunately, I have to take you to another spot that is just as peaceful, but most are less excited about visiting . The setting is a grassy, shade tree–lined park with small asphalt paths. It is usually quiet, with gentle breezes passing through the trees and rustling the leaves enhanced by the melodic chirping of a multitude of birds. It looked empty until I turned around to survey the entire area more closely and saw the multitude of headstones of many shapes and sizes and ages arranged in patterns, marking the final resting places of so many friends and loved ones.

I arrived early with my family, which included my wife, Mary, and our daughter and sons, all crowded into one car. All of us were saddened and not speaking, none looking forward to today's obligation. After exiting the car carefully, we slowly walked over to the grave site, still eerily silent due to our early arrival.

After several minutes of tranquility, I could hear the sound of young boys at play. It looked like a baseball game was about to start in a clearing adjacent to the cemetery. The boys chatted encouragement mixed with some good-natured insults. None were in uniform, for shorts or long pants, various T-shirts, and various baseball caps representing pro or school teams were their dress of the day.

They were of grade school age, and some looked as if they had not yet bathed for the day or had been hard at play gathering dirt on their clothing over time. Their communication was poor at times, suggesting that they were not from educated families. They did not lack enthusiasm for the game, for sure. It seemed each one was trying to show the other that they belonged here, on their team, even if they were the last pick for their side.

Soon, I heard in the background the sound of automobiles, a few and then more arriving for the funeral. Car doors opened and closed quietly. So many people were there that parking a distance away and walking to the grave site was required, regardless of the age of the mourners, young and old and in between. Most of them were white, and there were some blacks and Hispanics, wearing suits and sport coats and short sleeves and business dress and jeans.

All this activity attracted the attention of the ballplayers. The pitcher noticed first and, after staring initially, softly told the others to stop talking, then more strongly spoke to gain their attention. The players quietly gathered around the pitcher, facing the cemetery, with some removing their caps after a few minutes. All stood politely at attention—a pleasant surprise of respect for a group so young since not all fully understood what they were witnessing.

One of them finally asked, "What is it?"

The pitcher shrugged his shoulders initially, not clear about what he was seeing, but ultimately declared, "Oh, I know what is happening." It was now obvious, and he explained to all the ballplayers that this was a funeral, and the peaceful adjacent area was a well-kept cemetery where families and friends had come to honor and say their final goodbyes to their loved ones. He explained that he wanted them to be silent for now, at least till the funeral was done.

Chapter 2

IT WAS GETTING CLOSE TO NOON, AND THE HEAT OF THE day was building fast. As the crowd moved slowly from their cars to the graveside, I leaned over to my wife, stating softly, "I hate going to funerals and having to say goodbye! Always painful, but I suppose it is something we all have to endure." Clearly distracted, she ignored what I said.

I was unhappy to attend this but did it for the family's sake. I wore my favorite blue suit, although it was hot and uncomfortable. My wife stayed close to my side and next to our daughter and sons. She spoke to us about the location of the after-service luncheon, and reminded us that the funeral director would give out travel directions for the crowd that could make it. Not all would attend since some had to return to work after the service.

When the minister started talking, the group went silent. I felt the sadness in the air surrounding the group that now encircled the newly placed coffin shining in the late morning sun, and partially covered by some yellow, red, and white flowers, all so beautiful and so sad. Faint sobbing was heard, but not enough to make the painful experience worse than it already was.

The pitcher noiselessly left the field of play and gingerly approached me in the cemetery as I was standing next to my wife and family. I turned, leaned down, and whispered to the boy, "Good morning. Can I help you?" I could not ignore him for it appeared that he needed someone to talk to because of the troubled look on his face.

I put my arm around the young boy's shoulder and slowly moved him away from the crowd and over to a nearby shade tree to talk privately. He was about twelve, of fair complexion, sandy brown hair color and did not display any signs of acne, voice change, or facial hair. He seemed disturbed that a funeral was starting at the same time he was planning to have a fun day playing baseball with his friends. He was uncomfortable; this was very evident.

"Who is it?" asked the distraught young pitcher.

I said, "A dear friend that I have known for years. This is not easy for me or my family." My answers did not seem to reassure or comfort him.

The agitated boy continued, "But who are you?"

Over time my family would tire of my story telling that often was repetious, but now I was excited that I had found a new listener . I responded as obligingly as I could, "Well, I have been around a long time. And I remember when I was your age, I really liked playing ball games with my friends. Let's not worry ourselves about all those people over there. I will tell you my story to answer your question. So forget what you are seeing, and only pay attention to me, please, young man!"

Chapter 3

THE YOUNG BALLPLAYER REMINDED ME OF WHEN I was a twelve-year-old boy, running barefoot down a well-worn path in the woods with my ten-year-old sister in hot pursuit, playing hide-and-go-seek. We had done this so many times—clearing a path, crushing the grasses, and moving the sand—that we needed no map to follow through the woods. Both of us would sweat profusely from the summer heat, our bodies crusting salt and our churning feet kicking up dust onto our skin and clothes.

I told him, "Shoes were off for the summer. At least this was the case for my sister and me due to our family's lack of money, which allowed only one pair of new sneakers per year per child, which we put on only at the start of the school year. We would have to travel in Dad's old

Willys pickup truck, sitting in the back bed, bouncing about for miles all the way to the local farmers' market in Woodstown, New Jersey. Upon arrival, we were greeted with the distinct creature smells of the cattle, the carnival-like sounds of country music, and noisy crowds milling about, looking for a bargain at every table.

"At the shoe vendor, we would dig through piles of leftover shoes for our choice at the right price. We had to be cautious of mismatched shoes, trying to avoid a repeat of the time that Mom had bought me two left-footed white buck shoes for my first Holy Communion. The ill-fitting white suit, which was a hand-me-down from my older brother, was oversized, but it was my feet that killed me for no obvious reason throughout the service. At home later in the day, I took them off and told Mom of the error. Her unexpected response was 'What do you want for a dollar?' Thanks, Mom!

"Well, those secondhand sneakers had to last longer than the natural life of the purchase. Springtime at school was tough, for the holes would appear and the sneakers would fall apart, and classmates' laughter would start up again, along with their teasing. It was like a rite of spring. And, again, another schoolyard fight to protect my dignity and self-respect. And another stay-after-school penalty doled out by the teacher, but the late arrival home is what I dreaded the most! The leather strap was too easily used as punishment, often undeserved.

"Our mother, in her typical loud, commanding voice, would shout our names, telling us to return home *now*. We were the two youngest in a family of six and had two older brothers who ignored us and regularly biked into the small local town to play with their friends rather than play with us. Our brothers described us as *dumb* and several other unpleasant terms that I would rather not repeat. My sister, Dee, and I gained solace in each other's company. We enjoyed playing, talking, listening, and not judging each other.

"Once in the house, we were harshly instructed to wash up for a lunch meal. Ah, my favorite was peanut butter and grape jelly on white bread, but Dee would request a more substantial lunch, and often got her favorite of white bread with mayo and bologna. A clear sign of being Mom's favorite child. On this day, we had no cheese, since there was no money to buy it, but she was delighted to see her favorite olives as a side dish. They made her meal complete! Since the drinking water tasted so bad, the choice of powdered milk or coffee was very welcome to us, rather than eating our lunch dry.

"During the meal, we heard our father's truck door slam, and then he entered the home with the scent of cigarette smoke strong enough to partially mask the smell of alcohol. Though not clearly drunk, he was bubbly in conversation, which he often got when he drank too much alcohol. He never got mean when drinking, but would be quite likable, in a way.

"Dad would never yell or hit us with that infamous leather strap Mom wielded so freely. For company, he would ask my sister and me along for a drive in his Willys Jeep truck to 'anyplace but home,' according to him. It was a common temporary escape for him, and we were more than willing to oblige.

"Our mother and father were incompatible, like oil and water. They would start a verbal fight as soon as they saw each other. I knew it was difficult, if not impossible, to sustain a household of six with no job, no money, and often drunk . My sister and I heard this a million times from our mother, who would scream this fact during their nearly daily verbal battles.

"Dee and I would run from the kitchen up to the

security of the second floor and attempt to eat our food despite the intense shouting coming from the kitchen below. This conflict between the two of them was always the same—alcohol, lack of work and money—but sometimes, for periods of days or weeks, our father disappeared from the home for unexplained reasons. Upon his return, he would tell us he had been at 'a place to dry out and get back on the wagon.' That wagon idea made no sense till we got older and learned the true meaning of this from our classmates in school."

Chapter 4

"THE STORY, ACCORDING TO FAMILY LORE, IS THAT our father and mother met at a local church dance and started dating, and when Mother reached eighteen years old, they eloped to Elkton, Maryland, and were married by a justice of the peace. They stayed for a time in an old home owned by my mother's father before he built them a new home in Trainer, Pennsylvania. That eventually was my first home; I recall being raised there till age four, prior to our eventual move to New Jersey.

"Our mother was only sixteen when she had to quit high school, only completing ninth grade, so she could work at a local yarn mill to bring money home for her family during the Depression. She had little education, poor communication, no marketable skills, and a volatile personality, in my view. But what did I know? She would shout at us regularly, 'Children should be seen and not heard!'

"Kids always seemed to be a nuisance to her, and she made sure we knew it, including using that leather strap, especially on us boys, whenever she really got angry. Often, she was provoked by what we said, or we were too loud or did not move quick enough doing our assigned tasks. Sometimes, I felt it was our sheer existence that angered her. That is probably why our brothers often were away from the house.

"My father was raised in the Polish eastern section of Chester, Pennsylvania, and his food and clothing during those hard times were donated by the local Catholic church since my grandmother was a parishioner there. He only completed eighth grade since his parent (our grandfather, whom we had never met) died from tuberculosis and Dad had to drop out of school to find work, which was impossible in 1929, as the U.S. was in the throes of the Great Depression. Eventually, he altered his birth certificate, claiming he was eighteen, and lied about his mother's consent for him to join the U.S. Navy.

"Our father learned the trade of welding at a local

Chester shipyard after being discharged from the navy due to being underaged and lying on federal documents to get into the service. Grandmom (we called her Baba) had reported him to the U.S. Navy as underaged, and with forged documents, he was in trouble, with a criminal record that prevented him from getting good governmental jobs available to others.

"He resented that Baba did this to him. Like Dad, I could not understand it since no one was 'shooting at him' in the navy, as my father would often say. And it was safe and steady work and a good-paying job during bad economic times. As industrious as he was, his weakness and dependency on alcohol took him down regularly, unfortunately for us all. He went from job to job due to absenteeism from his steady drinking.

"My grandpop Dumen (Mom's father) was a Ukrainian conscripted into the Austrian Army overseas. And when his service was done, he left his wife and his two oldest sons back in the Ukraine and arrived alone in 1905 in Chester, Pennsylvania, where he worked by stoking coal into the ovens of the local electric factory. He was able to bring his family from the Ukraine by 1910. On his own time when not working, he learned masonry and carpentry skills. He borrowed money from the banks and built three small cottages near his home in Chester to generate a steady income for the family.

"With the market crash and the Great Depression, he lost those homes and had to return to the electric company, doing work no one else would do, which was common to immigrants. This was dangerous work and would eventually take its toll, causing him to die from lung cancer in 1947 at age sixty-three.

"After my parents married and had their first child, Michael, Grandpop and my father together built our first home in Trainer, with my father acting as an apprentice. That gave him skills that he would use in the future. Because of this, in 1949, my father took that uninsulated and unheated summer cottage in Bridgeport, with no running water or a bathroom, and created a fine family home with the help of all of us, including this seven-year-old 'assistant helper.'

"Actually, my job would best be described as 'runner,' tasked with locating and retrieving what Dad needed to do the job—limited, of course, by my age. These times were important to me, for I got to spend the most time of any of the family members with him. That made me feel important, and I know he liked my company."

To my surprise, the young fellow asked me, "You liked your dad a lot, didn't you?" This made me think about all his faults as a person and parent. Yet, despite all of them, I enjoyed being with him. There was a joy to all of this and a positive bond between us.

Chapter 5

"OK, BUT WHAT HAPPENED WITH ALL THE FIGHTing by your parents?" asked the little ballplayer, who seemed to be trying to help me focus on the story I was telling.

"Well," I said, knowing that I was losing my train of thought and I wanted to keep his interest in my story, "despite the clamor downstairs, my sister and I got our sandwiches down, with difficulty. Soon, the fighting was done, and the house grew quiet. We could hear our mother sobbing. We heard the front door slam shut and knew our father was leaving. Looking out of the upstairs window, we saw him get into his truck and drive off to where he felt he could 'find peace.' 'Probably to hide in a bottle,' as Mom would often say to describe his behavior. Well, he certainly had no help at home if he needed to escape his personal demons. But I was only twelve years old, so what did I know?

"My sister and I slowly re-entered the kitchen to check on our mother and saw her holding her head in her hands and softly sobbing. We moved to comfort her with our touch. But as soon as we spoke, she suddenly opened the gas oven door, turned on the gas, and placed her head and shoulders in the oven. We reached over to pull her back out, away from the stove, to show her we cared. 'No, no, Mommie, please don't do this!' We were so scared she would hurt herself and we would be alone! But this was not the first time she did this behavior that was traumatic to watch.

"I remember she would scream at us in anger, saying, 'You kids, I should have drowned you in the creek when I had the chance!' My sister would begin to cry, again. Poor thing! She was only ten years old and should not have to see and hear this. This was not fair to us, but I knew Mommie did not mean it. She said it so often when angry that we were numb to hearing it and did not really think she wanted to hurt us. But in the backs of our minds, we wondered if she would actually do it. I could not understand why a mother would ever say this to her children. What did we do wrong?

"I eventually returned to my bed upstairs to gain my composure, blocking my fears after another failed attempt to soften the family conflict over which I had no real control, yet I was part of the 'cause' of this constant fighting. Both my sister and I were not able to stop this cycle of conflict of our parents—always predictable, almost daily. But we did notice that an 'undeclared time-out' occurred between them around Christmastime every year. It was like a truce during war, which did make Christmas a time of the year that we looked forward to for the temporary peace and harmony and not for any material gifts, which were few and far between, anyway.

"Our home life was not like what I would hear described when talking to my friends at school. Ours was a different home life than what other kids talked about, so I never let them know what we experienced. My friends' family lives included dinners together, parents not arguing daily, brothers who played with brothers and sisters. At least that is what I heard them talk about, since Mom never allowed me to visit any of my friends' homes, for uncertain reasons. Our father never directed our upbringing, as he struggled with his alcoholism."

"Wow, both your mom and dad really had big problems!" noted my fascinated young listener. I was shocked by this observation by one so young, and I was energized to continue the story. I tried not to let his questions break my train of thought.

"Tell me more about your mother," pleaded the young ballplayer. Finally, I had an audience who wanted to listen. My family would often say, "We heard that one," just to shut down my storytelling.

"When I was four years old, while we lived in Trainer, Pennsylvania, prior to our move to New Jersey, I was asleep in the bedroom that my sister and I occupied together. I was suddenly awakened by my parents' screams coming from the kitchen. I groped my way through the darkness to the kitchen door, and upon opening it, in the bright lights, I saw in front of me my two brothers were crying hysterically.

"I then looked to my right to see my father holding my mother and her heavily bleeding right arm. Both were screaming at each other, and the large volume of bright red blood on my mother was so frightening that it was making me sick, and I started crying, frightened about whatever had happened. Daddy yelled to my two brothers to go away and take me back to my room with them.

"I could not sleep the rest of that night, and the next day, I begged my father to tell me what happened and tell me Mommie was OK. He told me she cut her arm on a five-gallon paint can with its lid open in the kitchen. She was taken to the emergency room and got stitches to stop the bleeding. I still did not really understand what had happened, but was not allowed to ask any more questions.

"Years later, in high school, I read of stories of suicide attempts by cutting one's wrist with a knife, and then it all made sense. After speaking to one of my brothers years later, he confirmed this."

"'That is a frightening story. I do not know how I would be able to watch that happen if one of my parents did it. I think I would never forget it either!" The young boy's eyes were wider than ever, and he begged me to continue my story.

Chapter 6

"I HAD A TOUGH START TO MY SCHOOLING, WITH MY stuttering that I had for kindergarten and the first two years of elementary school. As I mastered the basics of 'rithmetic, and writin', the more difficult skill of readin', especially out loud, improved exponentially, as did my confidence in school.

"I enjoyed the improving mastery of my schoolwork. I often finished among the five best students in the small class of twenty or so. Some school friends noticed this and made positive comments to me, which easily drove me to continue. Besides playing together, I and a few of the boys and girls that I initially met studied together all through elementary school, up to and including eighth grade, which was a help to all.

"Because of the distance from our home to the town and school, I only got to see them when school was in session, which I really enjoyed. Our mother would never let any of them visit our home, or allow us to play at their homes. Their lives were worlds away from our life at home that I could only imagine.

"As a downside, 'staying after school' was more common for me than I, my teachers, and my mother would have liked. I remember the episode in sixth grade when a student next to me was teasing me unmercifully about my torn sneakers. I should not have stood up in class, confronted him, and knocked him to the floor with one punch. It felt good when I did it, but it's not good to do this in the middle of a morning math session. Both of us had a lack of self-control, so I was pleased that James had to stay late as well since 'it takes two to cause trouble,' as Miss Jones would say. Getting home late meant Mom was there at our door, waiting for an explanation that was never adequate to prevent that leather strap from making an appearance. But by the next morning, I was able to sit down comfortably without any pain.

"Our school was in rural South Jersey in a farming district. It provided for our basic learning skills, but its physical plant was lacking, including no indoor plumbing. But

by fifth grade, the township had built a new school with
bathrooms not requiring the use of outhouses, which was
always a painful experience in the middle of a bad win-
ter with ice and snow, or even rainstorms in the warmer
months."

My little ballplayer was not sure what was worse, en-
countering the leather strap or having to use the outhouses
in the winters. I assured him that both were only transient
setbacks. Physical pain and scars will heal, but some emotional scars never go away!

"Conflicts continued at home, which contrasted with
the harmony (most days) in school that always gave me a
bright outlook for the future—at least my future! This was
in stark contrast to the pessimism that I often heard from
some of my family members.

"When my eighth-grade graduation day finally arrived,
my mother reluctantly agreed, after much begging on my
part, to attend the service; otherwise, there would be no
family there for me. Mom consented to go only after I in-
formed her that my school performance had been so good
that on the last day of class, our teacher said a number of
awards were going to be given to us graduates, so parents
should be there!

"Graduation was held in the basement of the local Methodist church in the center of town, which had the only venue large enough to hold twenty-five students, our teachers, and the families of the graduates. There was seating only for the graduating students.

"It was a very hot and muggy night in June 1958. Mom and I walked the one and a half miles to the church quietly, not speaking, which was common for her since she lacked good language and social skills and certainly was less outgoing than most people. When we arrived, we were sweating from the heat of the long walk from home into town.

"The church basement was very warm and crowded, with standing room only for guests, and my level of anxiety built up quickly as the ceremony slowly got to the awards presentation. Over thirty minutes, the ten awards for our small class were announced and distributed. Unfortunately, I received no award that night, despite my grand expectations. None at all! Not even the last one, for 'most improved,' which was the one I knew I richly deserved.

"Across the room, I could see my mother's angry face in the small crowd of parents. And the walk home was eerily silent; the tension was palpable. Finally, when she spoke,

I wished the trip home had stayed a silent one. 'You said you were going to get awards tonight, and you made me go to that terrible goddamn church. Nothing, nothing! You are as stupid as your brothers. You boys are going to amount to nothing!'

"Still angry, she then said, 'Kids are nothing but trouble, all of you!' The *nothings* seemed endless on that long, dark walk home since the sun had now set. Oh, how I prayed for the earlier quiet. I certainly wished that nobody had come to my graduation ceremony that night, especially my mother. I wished that *I* had not gone to that graduation!

"Back home, I quickly ran upstairs, dreading that the leather strap might make its appearance. I lay in bed in the quiet, in the dark, thinking about my elementary school years and tonight's disaster. Downstairs, the regular combat started up again, with the screaming between my parents. I had hoped my school performance would be a positive issue for them—that it would be the one thing they did not have to fight over. But it was clear to me that had not happened. It certainly did not help our family that night! This was just another nothing day among many for our family."

Chapter 7

"Now, I knew high school was going to be different. I could feel it in my nervous bones! We had to be bussed north to attend school in a consolidated district. Classes there were tough, and demands on my time to perform well academically meant minimal social time.

"Because I studied alone for hours, weeks, months, and years in the attic, I had my father set me up with an inexpensive desk from Sears, which I had to put together with his help. Mom allowed one of my fellow students access to our home on occasion for the purpose of studying only. Of course, we were monitored for compliance in this matter. Later in life, we would joke that by this cross-tutoring method, we helped each other succeed. The story we told was that he graduated in the bottom and I finished in the top of our class, and he became a millionaire and I became a medical doctor.

"I felt the reward of academic success through compliments from fellow students, teachers, and family, especially my sister, Dee. But tensions persisted at home with my father's continued unemployment, and our low family income created enormous hardship.

"Regularly, our cousin Paul was sent to visit us from Pennsylvania. He would arrive on the local ferry weekly, often with two bags of food under his arms from our aunt and uncle, who owned a bar in Chester. As one person, he could never consume this volume of food, so it was obvious why he was sent to 'visit.' Even I understood his importance to our family. Without this lifeline, it was not certain that our household could have sustained a family of six and remained together for as long as we did.

"On a rare occasion, my high school friends would convince me to take a break from schoolwork and offer me a ride back to the high school for dances, after which a few of the songs would keep circulating in my brain. I thought they were great rock 'n' roll songs, despite my father's warnings of the 'dangers' of this kind of music. If one of my older brothers had this music playing, he would shut it off and chase them out of the house to go play with their friends in town.

"Wow, this guy Elvis was amazing and his music made you want to sing and dance just like my black classmates! We kids all loved it and often sang the songs on the long bus rides to and from school. Our dad was worried *music* was a danger to us? How about our poverty, or his drinking, or his and Mom's daily fighting!

"I was very upset when my oldest brother, Michael, left high school after eleventh grade for the Air Force. Then three years after that, my brother Joey did the same and joined the Marines. Neither completed their high school education. I realized only later what the arguing and fist-fighting between my father and my two older brothers were all about. They were both forced to leave home and join a military service to help out the family financially.

"My sister and I recognized our brothers were sent away so that we were protected, like our father had left home as a sixteen-year-old to join the navy and send money to Grandmom so she could care for his two young brothers in Chester after his father's death. Well, our brothers never got to finish high school and certainly were not college bound, and the military was a good source of job training and income.

"Reluctantly, Dee and I accepted that this was how some families survived, but we felt very guilty that our family had to be broken up because of us. As much as our brothers were not nice to us, we felt the pain and guilt of their loss."

The young listener sensed the pain of this in my voice and said, "You know, sir, it was like your father did what he thought was best to make sure you and your sister were cared for and could get the schooling you needed. He did the best he could to help."

Maybe so. I could think of other ways to handle that, but I kept this to myself. I did not want to be argumentative and lose my best listener.

Chapter 8

"GRADUATION CAME QUICKLY. I FINISHED WELL academically, and I got financial help for a college education, which would create one less mouth to feed at home. At least this was the case during the school year—a full financial ride at a regional university, with its beautiful campus within a college town. And it was only an hour's ride from home, which meant my family (besides my brothers) could visit easily. Finishing at the top of my class was the ultimate experience for a kid who was to be the first family member to graduate from high school in fifty years, and with plans for college. I was very excited, and before I went, we planned to celebrate this rare achievement, or at least it was rare in our family.

"After the awards ceremony at my high school

graduation, I traveled home for a party planned by my favorite aunt, Mary, at our home. Arriving home, expecting congratulations from Mom, I was told that when young Anthony Z graduated high school (Mrs. Z was Mom's only childhood friend), he got more awards than I, and I was a disappointment and should have done better!"

"'You can't be serious! Your mother seems to be a very unhappy person and takes it out on her family," noted my ballplayer in disbelief. "So what did you say?"

"I just turned around and walked out of the house in front of my family, including my poor aunt and uncle, who had brought the food and cake for this small celebration to our home. I got into the family car and drove off, not staying for any party. I drove around aimlessly for several hours, till midnight, then returned home, which was now empty of all guests, and went up to the solitude of my bedroom upstairs, avoiding any family contact. I was angry at my mother, thinking that she would never be satisfied, regardless of what others did to please her and what they gave her and the family to be proud of as rewards for all her sacrifices as a parent. It was just another bad day for the 'stupid one' in our home."

"It seems that your sister was often a big part of your

life at home, at least till you went to college. Am I right?" said my young ballplayer.

"You are very correct since she and I experienced the same difficulties and were able to commiserate and support each other through many bad days. We listened to each other and counseled ourselves, despite our young age. Boy, did I miss this when I went off to college, since she had no understanding of what I was going through. They were tough times for me."

Chapter 9

"GETTING AWAY FROM THE TROUBLES AT HOME AND going to college was to be a thrilling yet stressful adventure, for I knew this was my stepping stone to have any chance of postgraduate education. I expected it to be very challenging, with much time spent with my head in the books. I was ready for the sacrifice of time needed to be spent and the pressure to achieve any goals.

"My sister, Dee, and I had talked about our futures often as we grew up and knew that education was going to be our ticket out of poverty. She was an average but hardworking student, but much better than the poor students that our two brothers were. She and I could confide in each other through the years while together at home. We respected each other's opinions. She ultimately went to

X-ray technology school in Philadelphia after I left home. It was a struggle for her, but she made it after much sweat and tears.

"On the occasional Sunday, my parents and Dee would arrive in the 'new' used Chevy and would escort me to the newly opened McDonald's in Newark, Delaware. It was like an ice cream stand, except I would get some of the best cheeseburgers ever, and chocolate shakes with fries, and still get change from a dollar!

"I had chosen the premed course of study although I knew few made the cut. But with my interest in science, especially biological science, I felt that I might financially be able to care for myself, and help the family as well, if I stayed the course for a career in medicine. My parents instead wanted me to be a teacher and forgo the prolonged and expensive education that the family could not afford.

"I wanted to show them that I could do something very few could ever achieve and become a doctor. Many in the family had not graduated from high school, let alone dreamed of college or professional school. This was for everyone, but especially for me. Nothing was going to stop me.

"During one of my first classes as a freshman, a female classmate came to my desk and asked to borrow an extra pen, which I did not have, nor did I want to befriend a girl. There was no way a girl was going to sidetrack my education plans, so I cautiously avoided providing any hint of interest.

"She had the prettiest blue eyes, and I think she had blond hair, but I noticed that some days, it was shaded differently. Despite my immediate unwillingness to create any social contact, I recognized that she was very attractive. And of all the kids in class, she asked me for help. Was I dumb not to offer help? Sorry, no potential distractions allowed!

"During my freshman and sophomore years, I would see her in the dining hall, for she was housed in an adjacent dorm. Despite my initial hesitation, months later, I went to her dorm during our sophomore term and nervously asked her out for a date. She quickly said no and said she had a boyfriend and was *pinned* with his frat pin from his college. I think that meant she was committed and not interested.

"I was crushed and embarrassed, uncertain about what to say next. I mumbled some words and said something like 'I am sorry to bother you' and left her dorm lounge awkwardly. I kept thinking, *Why did I make a fool of myself in thinking she would want to see me just because she wanted to borrow a pen?* I was so stupid!

"As I thought more about it, I did not know where we would have gone on a date if she had said yes. But it was like a relief she said no, although I could imagine it would have been wonderful if she had said yes. Certainly, it was for the best that she said no, I think.

"Sometimes, I would see her in passing on campus on the way to our classes, and I would say a muffled hello. Actually, I don't think it was loud enough to hear. Anyway, the rules were the rules, and pinned girl, no date."

"It seems to me that she made an impression on you," observed the youngster. Wow, for a twelve-year-old, he did not miss much.

"Thoughts of the incident would surface occasionally, but I knew that I could not push myself on her. She had her plans and I had mine. My goal was to get into medicine, and it was all-consuming! The stress level was very high, and I would often take isolated walks through the campus just to clear my head, letting me continue despite the unrelenting academic demands, with no distractions allowed! I wish I could have talked to my sister about all this confusion to sort things out in my head.

"One day in November 1963, I was resting in my dorm room between exhausting classes, which included a lot of demanding lab courses, when I suddenly heard another student running down the hallway, shouting, 'The president has been shot!' I jumped up and ran downstairs to the TV room to check this out. President Kennedy had been nearby only a week or so before to dedicate the opening of the Delaware Turnpike that was to be the new addition as part of U.S. Route 95 from Florida to Maine.

"The large number of students in our dorm gathered in front of the TV in the lounge and watched the sad and frightening event unfold. A youthful leader with much charisma was lost, and a future with so much potential was ended. Even Walter Cronkite's voice broke at times describing the event. JFK 'paid the price of sacrifice' to achieve what he wanted in fame and fortune and now was suddenly gone. So quickly, so violently. During this American crisis in leadership, we all prayed that our nation would come together to continue successfully.

"I quietly thought to myself that I hoped my sacrifices would pay off since some pay a very high price for high goals that they set. But my personal plans were more achievable, in my estimation!"

Chapter 10

"ONE DAY DURING MY SOPHOMORE YEAR, I WAS exiting a class when I ran into a freshman girl who attended one of my other classes, but whose name I could not remember. So she reintroduced herself as Valerie. While we were walking together for a short distance, her brother rushed up to her to talk about the political platform he was proposing as part of his plan to run for junior-year class president. After several minutes, he turned to me to discuss the matter, presenting the very same ideas to me that I just heard.

"I apologized, and said, 'Look, I am only a sophomore and can't vote for you. Besides, I have a lot of studying to do and have to go!' I ran off thinking, *Some people think they can make it in politics. Incredible.*

"Mumbling to myself all the way back to my dorm, I considered how so few make politics a successful career. My thoughts were then of my next class and not his plans. Little did I know that years later, he would be successful enough to become president of the United States. You never know who you might unexpectedly cross paths with.

"College was 100 percent a head-in-a-book approach, no time to even look up or come up for air. By my senior year, only 20 percent of my class made the cut. All of the remaining few got into med school, except for the one that decided, at the last minute, she wanted a PhD program in biology instead.

"I had two faculty interviews at Hahnemann Med School in Philadelphia. The first was with a pharmacologist, who said, 'You are from New Jersey and should not apply here, but apply to Rutgers in New Jersey instead!' *Oh my, did I make an error in choosing this school?* I thought as uncertainty now crept in. *Maybe I need to rethink my future plans.*

"As luck would have it, I was given a second interview a month later provided by a staff psychiatrist. When he said, 'Hello. How are you feeling?' I wondered, *Why is a psychiatrist interviewing me, and why did he ask me that question?* All I remember of this day is that I was so excited during my second-chance interview that my mouth and face hurt afterward from smiling so broadly. I remember shaking his hand, and then I left the school to catch the train from Philadelphia back to Newark, Delaware. This ordeal worked out for me in the end.

"A painfully long month later, I got the acceptance to med school I dreamed about. I had made the cut that so few achieve, and now I had the chance to study medicine, but no financial aid this time. A few more years of schooling and some postgraduate years as well—it seemed like an endless path of education. But I was ecstatic with this news.

"I traveled back home from college that weekend, for I had also received a postgraduate microbiology fellowship to Rutgers on the same day. This was fully funded with teaching obligations, in contrast to the medical school position that was all out-of-pocket costs. The length was the same, at four years, but I would become the teacher and not the doctor. I would be at the bench and not the desk. I would use a microscope and not a stethoscope. I would focus on bugs and not humans.

"So, I went back home for the weekend to help myself

decide my future. After a few walking trips to the local creek and the local farm where I had worked the past summers, I decided, 'It was med school first. I'll stay the course, with the lab and classroom as my backup!' I needed that peace and quiet at home, watching the gentle ebb and flow of the tide, to relax me and allow me to make that final decision without distractions.

"I had to discuss this important decision with Dee. She was now a practicing X-ray tech at the Philadelphia VA hospital and was as excited as I was about this. We had talked about college and medicine since we were in high school together and both of us selected a future in healthcare."

My young, keen listener blurted out, "It is no surprise that she was the one you would confide in since you did that for each other, growing up together."

I responded, "Yes, we helped each other as best we could. Often, just listening was all that was needed.

"Finally, college graduation happened in the university stadium with family, which included Mom, Dee and her new fiancé, cousin Paul, and Aunt Mary, our guardian angel. Afterward, I kept searching the crowd of graduates, looking for the blue-eyed girl and maybe her 'pinned guy friend,' but with no luck. I just wanted to see what he looked like, but I should not have been doing that, for I was not part of her plans. I suspect she had her life plans in place already.

"Leaving college with that diploma in my hand was an exhilarating feeling, but the best was still to come."

Chapter 11

"DURING THE SUMMER OF 1966, ONE OF MY AUNTS was diagnosed with stomach cancer, and my mother and I visited her in the hospital in Chester, Pennsylvania. My aunt was gaunt, wasted, unable to eat, and on regular doses of pain meds, likely narcotics. She knew she was dying, but no one would speak to her about it—not the doctors, the nurses, her friends, or her family. She lay there in bed, alone. Professionals and visitors and loved ones were there, but she was all alone.

"'Tell me that I have cancer,' she pleaded. My mother's reply was about the weather, and her trip over from New Jersey, but never the answer that my aunt wanted to hear, needed to hear, yet feared to hear—that word, *cancer*! My mother would continue her monologue while my aunt withdrew more into herself, sobbing barely audibly in the otherwise peaceful state of the room. Peace for who? Not my aunt, for she was alone in a crowd that ignored her emotional needs. All alone and not at peace, yet. I remembered this for my future patients.

"In the fall, med school started, and it was a very busy and academically tough time with our demanding exams. I always felt that impending doom every time I took a college exam with the anticipation of what the final grade would be—awful, painful feelings. But I now sensed the exhilaration of being in the medical environment that I had fought so hard to reach just to get that chance to try to become a doctor. I was well prepared academically for whatever was thrown my way by the time I got there.

"I excelled in my gross anatomy lab as a freshman, and when my second year began, I could feel the word *doctor* creep into my persona: *I am going to make it and be the guy who is there to help that sick person. I am going to be the person that helps my family. The person that all will be proud of. The one that some might have doubted could do it, except for me. The one without my father's pessimism and bleakness of the future. The guy not stupid just because he could not get any award at his eighth-grade graduation—or high school graduation, for that matter!*

"As a second-year medical student, I joined a local judo club to control the stress related to my schoolwork. It was located across the street from the med school and was a great help to maintain the needed focus on my studies. Rarely, I would stop by some of the student parties near the med school, encouraged by some of my classmates, who literally would pull me away from my desk at our library.

"Sometimes, thoughts of that blue-eyed girl would surface, but I knew nothing of what she had planned, and I had not seen her since college. My mind was laser focused on that medical degree, and nothing was going to stop me.

"Mother had seen a cardiologist and was told she had 'right bundle branch block,' which I did not understand at that time was a relatively benign medical condition. But when I went to our library to do research on this, I found information suggesting it was not as dangerous as she thought. At the med school bookstore, I purchased a readable introductory text on cardiac assessment that is performed during a routine physical exam to help assess the patient's situation."

My ballplayer asked, "Did you talk to your mother about this?"

I told him, "I did, but said I would get back to her with more information later. I called Dee to fill her in on what I was doing to get more information and put her mind at ease.

"At this time, as both parents had aged, my sister chose to stay close and watch them for us. Well, *us* in this case was Dee and I since our brothers did not want to be responsible in any way for our parents. As problematic as our parents were, they were still our parents!

"Mind you, I knew very little about the heart. But I spent two consecutive nights reading that physical diagnosis book from cover to cover to lessen my anxiety about my mother's health, thinking that I could master the complex field of cardiology in two nights to help her. I had every word and page committed to memory despite having no personal clinical experience.

"A few days later, during clinical teaching rounds at the hospital, four students, including me, accompanied a staff clinician into the hospital to see patients and discuss clues for physical diagnosis at the bedside of a willing patient. For over an hour or more, the attending doctor and I cross-discussed cardiac physical diagnosis on opposite sides of the bed, with the patient between us. The patient was cooperative but amazed at all the detailed information exchanged by the two of us. We dominated the educational session, and it seemed that there was nothing the two of us did not know about the heart.

"The three other students silently stood nearby in the patient's room and seemed excluded from the lesson, as they could only listen, unable to interrupt the intense bedside teaching interaction of the attending doctor and me. It was like the clinician teacher and I were reading the same text verbatim, like a book was photographed in both our minds. We anticipated the questions and answers of the other, talking only between the two of us. At the end of the session, I was mentally exhausted but exhilarated!

"The other students looked incredulously at us, then quietly left the floor without comment. The clinician kept staring until he finally said, 'Thank you,' then hurried off to his other work duties since he was the hospital's chief of internal medicine and one of our major educators—unknown to me at that time—and one that I was to respect later in my professional education as one of the best clinicians I ever met during my medical career."

Chapter 12

"MY LAST TWO YEARS AT MED SCHOOL WERE FULLY clinical and exciting, like being 'almost a doctor,' and included surgical and medical rotations where we were exposed to many problems. The other students and I saw patients with the interns, residents, and attending physicians. It was an incredible experience. One noteworthy rotation was on the psych service; that I found challenging and very mentally exhausting. I developed more fatigue there than if I had been up all night covering night call for a medical or surgical specialty.

"On the last day of service, I submitted a psych analysis of myself using skills I had learned during the rotation. In addition, I chose to write about the topic of 'death in the family,' not expecting my family might soon be experiencing this very trauma. I handed in my work on the last day of service, then headed home that evening for Easter break.

"When I entered the house, to my dismay, I found my father looking very ill. He was 'sick with chest pains,' according to my mother. I pleaded with him to discuss his complaints and said I would take him to the emergency room for care.

"My efforts as a son and future doctor were dismissed. He vehemently refused to go, saying, 'If I go to the hospital, I will die!' His fears, chronic alcoholism, and inability to handle what life threw at him were on full display that night. Unfortunately for him and our family, his choice for his care to be delayed was not a smart one.

"I had difficulty sleeping that night, listening for any sound from my father's room. My parents slept apart, in separate rooms, for years, so he was alone in that room. I anxiously awaited any call for help, for I was more than ready if he reached out. All he had to do was ask. I wanted to be there for him even if he did not want it.

"Early the next morning, I found him dead in his recliner in his bedroom—alone and incapable of overcoming his fear to reach out and seek help from others, including his own family. He was not going to change, and now, he never would. *Denial, avoidance,* and *fear* best describe how my father conducted his life—courage from alcohol and not himself. And that is how he spent his last night on earth, in fear, unchanged to the very end.

"The self-analysis I provided and the 'death in the family' thesis I wrote described the loss of loved ones and how families handle it differently. In addition, I described as best I could my family's abnormal dynamics, my mother's emotional liability and lack of insight and sensitivity, and my father's alcohol dependency. Neither parent had enough understanding to help the other, and that left its scars on all of us.

"My mother had no understanding that her verbal and physical abuse to her children, especially her sons, was not the example to set when parenting. Her attitude toward her daughter was different, almost as if she was working our sister into the role of long-term caretaker for herself.

"It is no surprise that my oldest brother was briefly married but then divorced due to verbal and physical abuse of his spouse. My other brother, who was the ex-Marine and retired merchant seaman, never got married and only disparaged women, seeking never to be married.

"Both parents had personal and psychological needs that could have been handled professionally if only the family was not 'dirt-poor.' But they also needed to reach out for help from others, and clearly, neither one was ever going to do that.

"After Easter break, my psych director invited me to his office to interview me about my personal loss to console me. And, after reading my self-analysis, I suspect he wanted to be assured that I was stable enough to continue my medical school training, and show his willingness to provide personal support to me, if needed."

Chapter 13

"DESPITE STARTING MY SENIOR YEAR WITH THE loss of my father, I kept up the intensity needed to master my medical skills. A few fellow med students, who were planning to study and practice dermatology, radiology, or psychiatry, solicited me to cover their medical student night-call rotations in the hospital. They were not interested in doing medical call and losing sleep if their interests were not in general medicine.

"I was excited about the prospect of having more patient experience and getting paid by my fellow students for this chance. I demanded and got paid a whooping ten dollars a night, which attracted more requests than I could handle. But I loved it, for I did about twice the clinical work volume that any other student did that year. I felt that there was going to be little I had not seen or done by the time I was an intern. I was correct, as I found out later in my clinical years.

"Our chief of medicine, with whom I had that cardiac-physical bedside encounter during my second year of medical school, did discover this added medical student call schedule. He felt that paying not to be on call was hurting those students, so he was upset.

"I bravely defended myself, saying, 'Dr. Oaks, no way would I do something like that for any amount of money in the world! I know it would be wrong.' Well, I did not get into trouble, but I also did not stop the practice. I enjoyed every extra bit of work that was thrown my way.

"But forty years later, at Dr. O's retirement event in Philadelphia, I approached him to apologize. He said, 'I know you lied.' I was not certain he really remembered it, but I felt better, somewhat. When I did see that smile of his, I felt even better about my apology.

"In August of that last academic year, two of my med school classmates wanted me to go with them to a big out-door concert on a large farm in New York State that was to last for three days. I declined due to the extra workload that I had added, then found out later about their experience of being part of the massive crowds of young people coated in mud and soaked to the skin by heavy doses of rain, with and without clothes, and musical groups that would never be found in one location again. This was indeed a once-in-a-lifetime event—mud and music and youth in all their glory, so to speak.

"Well, I really was not sorry I did not go, for I had plans and was not getting distracted. Although this was a monumental event to many of my young peers, it was not important to me.

"As my senior year quickly passed, I loosened up a lot about socializing and went out on a date with the help of one of my fellow students. He set up a triple date, but the young lady with me would not dance, would barely speak to me, and, when I was dropping her off at the local nursing dorm, would allow only a limp handshake good night. Her boyfriend (another one, again) was in Harrisburg, and she only reluctantly went out with me that evening.

"Another student nurse on that triple date was pleasant and smiling and easy to talk to. I later saw Mary several times in the hospital cafeteria. I also ran into her at a local med student party. As I was 'wallpapering' myself, yet trying to look cool, she saw me and said, 'Want a beer?' We both had a great time talking about school that night.

"She was a senior nursing student about to finish up, just like me. Finally, I asked her for a date. We dated a couple of times during the final days of my senior year, going to the local pub and a movie. I remember she was attractive and had sparkling hazel eyes. I wondered if they sparkled for everyone.

"Then one day, she asked, 'About us?' Oh no, I knew what she was asking! The question really meant, 'Do we have a future together?' I really liked her a lot. I was very comfortable in her presence, for she had such a reassuring quality when she spoke. I was not certain what to say since I had never developed a relationship with anyone. I did know she was smart and would certainly make an excellent nurse, supportive and caring. Those eyes of hers were very beautiful.

"I'm not sure if this was the right thing to say, but I had an unsettled matter on my mind: 'Well, there is another girl.' It got very quiet, tears slowly welled up in her eyes, and she said, 'Oh.' I was not sure myself. I then quickly said, 'Maybe I will call you later.'

"We parted company slowly in front of her nursing

dorm, for both of us were unclear what was next in store. I rushed back to my apartment, rather upset about what had just happened. I had to get my mind straightened out, for things were now really mixed up. My sister was now married and had her own personal life, so I was alone on this one.

"I was at the end of my major education, with post-graduate education looming, and I had isolated myself from relationships for so long that I had no life outside of medicine. And it was very lonely, like sitting at the bar of a local pub for some food and beer by myself, very awkward and lonely. This had to change one way or another, for I wanted and needed this to stop."

"Wow, what did you do to get out of the mess that you created?" asked my inquisitive young man.

Brother, I did not need that stone thrown at me by this fellow who had very little life experience under his belt! But he was right-on about needing a plan.

Chapter 14

"LEAVING MARY THAT NIGHT, I FELT I HAD TO DEcide what to do next, for I suspected life was about to change in a major way. The next night, I got dressed in my well-worn suit (the only one I had), a tie (a skinny clip-on type), and an old trench coat, and after combing back my slick black hair, I walked to Philadelphia's Suburban Station and headed by train to Trenton, New Jersey.

"Years before, I had discovered that the blue-eyed girl was from Trenton, New Jersey, and her father had worked with the New Jersey State Police. I had found their home address the old-fashioned way, using the local yellow pages.

"Now keep in mind that I had never had an official date with her, had no direct communication with her for years, yet felt that I could not move on in my life without clearing up the unanswered question of her availability. So, I had waited almost four years to directly ask her about her feelings about us! Us? What was I thinking?

"I arrived by cab from the Trenton train station and knocked on the front door of her family's home. Her father opened it, not understanding the reason for the visit as I asked, 'Is Susan home? I would like to see her.' I then identified myself and said I knew her from college. Both her father and her mother appeared stunned standing in the doorway. Her mother was wearing an apron and holding a plate that she was drying with a kitchen towel, indicating that they had just finished dinner.

"After several minutes of stunned silence, her father politely invited me in and asked me to have a seat in front of their new color television. I had never seen a TV with such clarity and was easily distracted by it. I told him about this, almost forgetting why I was there. He asked again why I came. He left the family room and quickly returned with an album filled with photos of their daughter's wedding, dated four years earlier. It was 1966, and now, I was asking to see her in 1970 as if she had been waiting for me. He and I spent several minutes looking at the pictures while her mother quietly washed the remaining dishes in the kitchen, avoiding eye contact and not joining in our conversation.

"Finally, after enough of my questions, it was clear that what brought me there that night had been answered. Susan's father and I both stood up, and I thanked him and his wife for their time and apologized profusely several times, considering the unusual nature of the visit. Not much was accomplished except confirmation that it was definitely time for me to move on.

"I was about to leave to find a cab when Susan's father volunteered to give me a ride back to the local train station. He was so gracious and sympathetic and continued asking me questions during the ride. We stopped at a local bar that he frequented, where he knew a few patrons. We sat together at the bar and talked, and he said hello to some friends while we were there. Since the train back to Philadelphia was later that night, we had time to talk.

"He offered, 'Would you like a beer?' I said, 'Sorry, I don't drink, but sure would like a soda.' He was terrific, considering how strange it was meeting me for the first time. It was very unexpected, for sure. A young stranger arrived at their home at night asking about their married daughter, after having no contact with her since college. Very strange.

"He eventually gave me his business card that showed he worked for the New Jersey State Police and said if I needed anything, I should just give him a call. He was extremely kind to me that night, and I still think about him and that encounter.

"After parting company at the train station, I got onto the Philadelphia-bound train. The ride back to Philadelphia was a quiet one, with thoughts of this girl with whom I was infatuated but had never established a real connection. Yet I had been shocked and disappointed by the news of the visit. I was embarrassed for her parents and myself that I had visited them, but glad I had resolved the matter in my own mind and had to move on. I still had big plans for my future and a hopeful feeling about them.

"I eventually did get to see Mary again, but I now had to explain myself. She did a better job than I when she assessed the situation by describing the blue-eyed girl as my 'imaginary girlfriend.' This was painfully accurate when I first heard her say it. However, time did lessen the pain. One can't fool a smart nurse. And I found a very good one."

"'Wow, you really were off base, weren't you?'"

I did not know what to say next to my young listener, for his reaction made my story seem so awkward that I wanted to quickly talk about something else and stop the embarrassment.

Chapter 15

"I HAD JUST GRADUATED FROM MED SCHOOL, AND IT was now my time to be a real doctor. No longer a student, nor with interns or residents or attending physicians in front, it was me first! When the patients, families, and staff looked at me, they now said, 'What's next, Doctor?' Being on the front line of medicine is like going to battle with casualties potentially everywhere. You can't hesitate, for it could make a big difference in the outcome.

"My first clinical rotation was in the ER. Oh my god, it was the busiest, most hectic place to start an internship. I prayed for those extra night and weekend calls to pay dividends for me and my patients and give me the confidence that I could handle the pressure. Maybe having seen those situations in the past would make me able to address them quickly and confidently.

"So, at midnight, I quietly entered the emergency room from the hospital accessway, trying not to be too obvious that I was trembling inside, and trying to keep my heart rate down. I had been notified earlier that I was to see every single patient that arrived for care in the ER for the entire twelve-hour shift. I would be able to get support from the nursing staff and the clinical medical and surgical services that were available twenty-four seven. I was planning not to hesitate in asking for help while I was 'in charge.'

"I stopped and looked around and listened carefully. Ah, yes! Nurse Leslie was certainly the one that I earmarked to be my go-to staff member. She was in her early forties and spoke clearly, directed her staff with confidence, and was pleasant about it. Her smile was infectious, and she always looked you in the eye when conveying what she wanted done—like, now!

"The first shift in the early hours of the day was fine with me, for I thought it was likely to be quieter, with the volume of patients picking up as the new day began at daybreak. I forgot that we were a Center City hospital, and during the night, many crises would appear at our doorstep, like gunshot or knife wounds.

"This was unlike what I saw growing up in the farming districts of South Jersey, where I used to pick fruits and vegetables in the summer heat. The sound of a big green pepper exploding was fun, but not the mushy tomato that left a big red stain on your shirt and provided evidence to the farmer that you were not working in the fields. As farm workers, we were often subjected to a 'dressing down' since he had been an army captain in World War II.

"My first shift was busy, but with each patient, I gained confidence in what I was doing. I was exhausted but almost euphoric about my work. When I only had about three hours left in my shift, and the sun was now coming up for the new day, Leslie approached me about a new patient behind curtain number four. He was a local attorney who arrived early to his office across the street and sustained a two-inch laceration of the right forearm that needed stitches. Oh my, I had only done this once before and, worse, he was a lawyer! What bad luck for the both of us!

"My charge nurse reassured me, gave me the proper sutures and equipment, and gently pushed me through the curtain in the direction of that poor lawyer. Actually, the procedure went well, with the patient and I chatting and developing a connection that helped both of us through this emergency. He was very attentive as his eyes appeared wider than most when talking.

"Suddenly, Leslie shouted out with urgency in her voice, 'Doctor, I need you now behind curtain three!' She did not say what the problem was, but I understood I had better move quickly. I gently got up and excused myself, leaving in an unhurried manner to get to Leslie. I was shocked to see a middle-aged black man with a large, open chest wound, the lungs visible and moving as he breathed. He was in serious trouble and suffering. The surgeons call this a *sucking wound*, and it's likely to cause death if not treated quickly.

"Leslie grabbed my arms and jammed a large, clean pressure dressing into my hands, then forced them down onto his chest. 'Press and hold this over his wound very tightly, and do not move till I tell you!' I think I shook my head, letting her know I understood. I was speechless and I prayed that he did not die on my shift. I made sure that I did not stop breathing during this crisis. Within minutes, the surgical team was at the bedside and took over, rushing the patient to the OR to close the wound and save his life.

"After that patient was removed from the ER, I sauntered back to my lawyer patient to finish the laceration repair. His eyes now were wider than ever, looking double in size since I last saw him. 'How is the patient?' he asked anxiously. 'He is going to be just fine!' I said confidently to reassure myself.

"Two weeks later, the medical director of the ER received a letter of commendation about the lawyer's care in the ER despite all the sick patients there during his visit. He cited Nurse Leslie and me by name. I proudly commented, 'There was really nothing to it,' when the director presented a copy of the letter to me. This convinced me that the best line of defense in a medical emergency is a skilled nurse.

"While my shift was winding down, the staff told me about a derelict living on nearby Vine Street who needed medical care and had been brought in by the police. The staff told me they wanted to clean him up before I saw him. I peeked into the patient's room and saw an elderly black man who looked awful and smelled worse. I agreed that I would come back after he was cleaned up.

"When I returned, I was shocked to see that my patient (I called him Mr. X) was a white male after the dirt was removed. And he was middle-aged, not elderly. After the staff cut off his shoes, we saw that all his toenails had grown into the shape of the shoes, as they had been on his feet for years. On his right arm was a three-inch open wound exposing his forearm bones. It looked rather clean, as the maggots were effectively cleaning it for him. When Mr. X sat up, looked at me, and said, 'Where did you get that ugly tie, Doctor?' I excused myself and left the room to dispose of that brown clip-on tie that I had treasured for years, despite its coffee stains and probably other work-related matter on it.

"Now, Mary and I had been dating for a few months since my trip to Trenton, and she saw that tie every time I was in the hospital. She thought it was unclean and unsightly and had suggested that I get a new one. It took awhile for me to admit to her that I got rid of the tie, and the real reason that caused me to replace it. The deciding factor of Mr. X's opinion did bear a lot of weight in my new dress code.

"At noon that day, my intern replacement arrived but was walking very slowly and looking rather gray in the face. Stanley was not happy to be in the first group of interns placed in the ER for the academic year. His anxiety level was inappropriately extreme, but this *was* the most difficult position an intern could have at the start of their internship anywhere. I excitedly told him that today was going to be a great day for him. He did not believe me. I saw the doubt in his eyes.

"As I left Stanley for his baptism by fire, I told him to look for the nurse that he could depend on and to act like a barnacle on a ship, keeping her as close as possible. The best defense for the intern and the patient was a knowledgeable and caring nurse. I learned that early on, for sure.

"My relationship with Mary blossomed to our wedding in May near the end of my internship. We lived together in Philadelphia close to the hospital, then in southern New Jersey. We both worked at the same hospital, but eventually, she had to give up nursing to care for our new daughter. My schedule was so demanding that she could never return to that position as we went through my postgraduate years, and then two more youngsters were added within the next few years."

Chapter 16

"AFTER COMPLETION OF A RATHER DIFFICULT AND prolonged educational journey, I found a medical position back in southern New Jersey, having finished a two-year gastrointestinal training program at Yale in the south, then at UConn in northern Connecticut, outside of Hartford. Both Mary and I had planned to return to where our parents still lived.

"My new work location was a multi-specialty medical group of internal medicine doctors with the responsibility of our own patients and the added burden of night and weekend medical call for the attached hospital. It was a stressful job that was demanding mentally and physically till the hospital brought in its own physician house staff in the mid-1980s.

"In those years of 1975 to 1985, there were no radiological options like CAT scans, MRIs, or ultrasounds. Till the technology was created, clinical care was solely on the shoulders of the doctor and his training, judgment, and learned skill.

"The most difficult experiences that I had to endure were the emergency calls to the labor and delivery room in the maternity wing. At that time, our hospital had three thousand live births each year and was the busiest in the region. When a crisis happened, it usually was a disaster, and the medical service was called in to help as best we could in those days.

"I recall, in the first five years of my practice, getting called several times for these crises, with only one surviving with congestive heart failure. The others had massive pulmonary embolisms, acute myocardial infarctions, or cerebral bleeding from toxemia of pregnancy.

"One of these incidents occurred the day before Mary delivered our third and final child in 1978. She knew something was wrong, but I did not tell her the story until a week after her safe delivery. I still remember and feel the loss of the young mother and unborn child that day. And the poor expectant father's shattered look will not be forgotten.

"As advances in medicine helped us effectively treat patients, and outcomes improved, we could intervene in crises and make them better for the patient, the family, and the physicians. This was incredible for all of those we helped and sad for those we could not. Sometimes, comfort care for the patient may be the best we could humanly do for someone that was suffering, for we were still not able to save everyone.

"For the years that I spent practicing medicine, I was grateful for the chance to make a difference in people's lives, and I certainly think about those that I saved and those that I lost. Each one was someone's loved one— someone's father, mother, brother. I watched patients die who should not have died, with the care modern medicine could offer, and some survived in spite of the odds against survival, shocking the medical team and showing the resilience of the human body during the stress of life-threatening diseases. What an amazing journey."

Chapter 17

"Mary and I had a terrific relationship and three children who were growing very fast, which kept the two of us very busy. The practice was extremely busy, but I was not in a position of management yet, being only a 'junior partner.'

"But it was not over. Thoughts about the blue-eyed girl would sometimes recur, and seemingly were never satisfactorily answered, despite the encounter with her parents almost fifteen years earlier. I had never spoken to her directly, only briefly as a college student. So after several years in active medical practice in New Jersey, on a whim, I drove down to southern Delaware to look for the town where she had moved according to alumni records. She had a family and was teaching and doing school counseling. Her husband was a biology faculty member at the university.

"It was a quaint, small town with a few places to eat, and I was hungry from the long ride. I entered a local restaurant and sat down quietly. I thought about what to order, but more importantly, *Why am I here? What do I expect to happen next? Is there any chance of seeing Susan?*

"After my meal, I got up to walk to the boardwalk next to the restaurant and the beach. I was searching for something, but what? Unknown and unseen by me were a couple who watched me leave the diner, then followed me onto the boardwalk without initially approaching me.

"I walked to the boardwalk railing, staring at the wide, relaxing expanse of the ocean, enjoying the peaceful view after having made this strange trip. For what reason? I was ready to go back home, not sure of what I accomplished. The several hours of a tiring return trip awaited me. What a dumb idea this was! But the view was beautiful indeed, with the gentle slap of the ocean on the beach, the light breeze, and the moderate temperatures common at the shore.

"Suddenly feeling the presence of someone nearby, I spun around and was face-to-face with the blue-eyed girl from college! Now older but not showing the effects of working, teaching, raising children, and the responsibility of family life, she was just like I remembered her from college when she asked for that pen and later told me, 'No date'!

"Frozen in place, hoping for but not expecting this unplanned meeting, I said nothing initially. She spoke first, saying, 'I remember you from college. How are you doing? What brings you here?'

"'Well, uh, uh,' I said with authority. It was clear that she was in charge.

"She continued, 'You know one can't change history. It is what it is. Things happen in life for a purpose. I assume you are happy with a great wife and family? I am sure many good things await you down the road!'

"I finally got enough courage to say, 'I always wanted to thank your mother and father for letting me have that unexpected visit to your home!'

"She looked at me and laughed. 'Yes, that was a surprise, wanting to visit me and ask me out for a date years after I got married, had children, worked as a teacher, and had not heard from you in any way for years. It was very strange!'

"I started to say apologetically, 'I am so—'

"She interrupted, 'No, no, they were good about it, but they chuckled when they called to tell me what happened. I am here now with my husband, so I have got to go, but safe travels back home, and thanks for visiting us. You know, this was a beautiful story, so don't try to change it.'

"She then turned to walk back to her husband, who stood on the boardwalk in the distance, and when she approached him, he embraced her gently. I watched them briefly but turned away. My mouth was very dry, and I almost choked on my tongue. While she was hugging her husband, they began slowly walking. She was right. It was time to leave for home.

"Was this meaningful or just a casual encounter like in the past when we first met? So much occurs that we don't understand and often miss when dealing with relationships. But did she and I ever have one? Certainly, we both had definite plans for our futures when our paths briefly crossed, but they did not include being together.

"When we make choices at the many diverging paths in our lives, can we ever be certain that they are the right ones? One really can't go back and change things. I think things happen for a reason."

Chapter 18

"THE DRIVE HOME WOULD BE A FEW HOURS OF quiet filled with thoughts of my past, present, and future. I had experienced a connection with my past that I could not erase and needed to understand more about. Maybe it was an infatuation at a watershed time in my life—maybe yes, maybe no! Certainly time was no longer on our side and our life stories were nearly fulfilled.

"After starting back on the road, I noted a sign pointing to the Cape May–Lewes Ferry, and did an abrupt U-turn and headed to the Delaware Bay to grab a ferry ride to New Jersey, hoping for more time to digest what had just happened. It was really crazy, but this encounter was helpful in reminding me that I needed to move on. It was not unlike the trip to her family home in Trenton when I was a senior medical student. The answer to my question had not changed.

"The ferry transported cars and people between Lewes, Delaware, and North Cape May, New Jersey. It was an eighty-five-minute trip and a lot of fun to ride. It reminded me of my youth, when we would travel from Bridgeport, New Jersey, to Chester, Pennsylvania, on the ferry that was replaced in 1974 by the current Commodore Barry Bridge, which was the largest cantilever bridge in the U.S. at that time. It was a relaxing experience then, and it was now.

"As the ferry left the dock in Lewes heading to Cape May, I stood at the back of the ferry, smelling the diesel fuel as the two four-thousand-horsepower engines pushed the ferry forward with awesome power. I kept staring at the shrinking town of Lewes and the boat slip. It was appropriately symbolic that my vision of the past was disappearing, and when it was no longer visible, I moved to the front of the vessel, looking forward to try to focus on all the good things I'd experienced and all the things still to be in my future."

"Whatever happened to your sister, who you spoke about earlier?" asked the wise young baseball player. "She and you seemed to have an important bond while growing up."

I was not excited about this question, but I had to answer it for him. "Well, I lost her a couple of years ago, despite her being younger than I. She suffered from lung disease, and those final few months of her life were painful to watch for her family as well as me. When I saw her at the viewing, she was peaceful and comfortable for the first time in quite a few months. Although I could not talk to her, I knew what she would be saying to us about our clothes, our behavior, or things that would bother her.

"She and I knew that we helped each other get through tough times growing up and then had our own families to take care of, with all their burdens, their highs, and their lows. We found others that we could connect with and communicate with and that could help us along in life. But we did OK for ourselves and our loved ones, hoping to lead by example for others. Now, whenever I get offered olives at meals, even if only in a martini, I always think of her!"

Chapter 19

THE YOUNG BALLPLAYER WAS MESMERIZED BY MY story, and he almost certainly had not expected all this personal information from a complete stranger. He remained silent, attentively listening throughout my storytelling, except for his occasional questions.

I spoke again. "What a crazy story, huh? Well, like I said, I married that student nurse with the great smile and sparkling green eyes that I met on that triple date. Mary gave up her nursing career so we could have three great children, and later, six wonderful grandchildren. She made a lot of sacrifices caring for the kids while I was at work many days, nights, and weekends. She managed the household with a firm, loving hand.

"But after fifty-three years in medicine, I retired to

enjoy life and let the doctors care for me rather than the reverse. Time for me to get the help that I gave out for years to others."

When I looked up amid my story, I saw the crowd was slowly dispersing, with people going back to their cars to leave. "Oh no, the service looks like it is done! And I missed it all!" I exclaimed.

As the boy and I both got up from beneath the shade tree, I said to him, "I got so distracted that I need to find Mary so we can proceed to the funeral luncheon together. Thanks, young man, for listening to the story of an old man. I hope there was a lesson in it for you. Please, take care, and I hope to see you again in the future."

Chapter 20

QUICKLY, WE SEPARATED AS HE RAN BACK TO HIS friends and I rushed over to my family. As I walked up to my car, the door closed on me and the car moved off, leaving me standing there, by myself. Alone! All alone, as if I did not matter anymore.

Where is Mary? Wait, I have things to say and plans that are unfinished for the two of us! And the kids and grandkids will grow up, and I need to be there to celebrate with them.

Suddenly, I heard that young voice, again. It was the pitcher. "Mister, you want to play ball with us now?"

I turned and saw the ball field where the boys had patiently been watching the funeral and waiting for it to end. I walked over to them, not sure what was happening when the pitcher handed me the ball.

Slowly, I realized what this meant and said, "It looks like it is my turn to pitch." I adjusted my cap, brushed off the dust on my pants, and made sure the shoestrings of my well-worn sneakers (holes included) were tied so I didn't trip and fall when running, still feeling numb to what had just happened. I thought about all of this, thinking, *I had a great life. I'm grateful, and happy that at least I still get to play ball with my friends.*

The view of the ball field and cemetery grew smaller as the ballplayers continued to play and their voices slowly weakened. The cemetery was gradually vacated of mourners as it once again became peaceful. The scene returned to the restful image of the wetlands of a quiet southern New Jersey swamp and waterway loaded with water lilies, slow-moving currents, and the sounds of croaking frogs and crickets. This was my home, where I could finally get rest.

About the Author

John M. Noldan was born in Chester, Pa and raised dirt poor in the farming districts of Southern New Jersey. Born into conflict at home but flourished in school nurtured by teachers and schoolmates. When graduating high school in 1962, he proudly became the first one on all sides of his family to do so since they entered the US in 1905.

After 53 years as an active licensed practitioner of Medicine, he retired but not his desire to write. This novel is fictionalized and semi-autobiographical but ideas surface each day to help put into words for the reader to be able to visualize and feel what the everyman does as he matures. So common yet unique of an experience that we all identify with it in some way.

Printed in the United States
by Baker & Taylor Publisher Services

Printed in the United States
by Baker & Taylor Publisher Services